Sit Down

Luke 10:38-42
(Mary and Martha)

by **Mary Manz Simon**
Illustrated by **Dennis Jones**

CPH.
SAINT LOUIS

Books by Mary Manz Simon from Concordia Publishing Hou

Hear Me Read Level 1 Series
What Next?
Drip Drop
Jibber Jabber
Hide the Baby
Toot! Toot!
Bing!
Whoops!
Send a Baby
A Silent Night
Follow That Star
Row the Boat
Rumble Rumble
Who Will Help?
Sit Down
Come to Jesus
Too Tall Too Small
Hurry Hurry!
Where Is Jesus?

Hear Me Read Big Books Series
What Next?
Drip Drop
Send a Baby

Follow That Star
Sit Down
Come to Jesus
Too Tall Too Small
Where Is Jesus?

Hear Me Read Level 2 Series
The No-Go King
Hurray for the Lord's Army!
The Hide-and-Seek Prince
Daniel and the Tattletales
The First Christmas
Through the Roof
A Walk on the Waves
Thank You Jesus

Little Visits® Series
Little Visits on the Go
Little Visits for Toddlers
Little Visits with Jesus
Little Visits Every Day

Stop! It's Christmas
God's Children Pray
My First Diary

Copyright © 1991 Concordia Publishing House
3558 S. Jefferson Avenue, St. Louis, MO 63118-3968
Manufactured in the United States of America

Library of Congress Cataloging-in-Publication Data
Simon, Mary Manz, 1948–
     Sit down : Luke 10:38–42 : Mary and Martha / by Mary Manz Simon; illustrated by Dennis Jones.
     p. cm.—(Hear me read Bible stories)
Summary: Retells for the beginning reader the Bible story about Mary and Martha.
     ISBN 0-570-04701-3
     1. Bible stories, English—N.T. Luke. 2. Jesus Christ—Friends and associates—Juvenile literature. 3. Mary, of Bethany, Saint—Juvenile literature. 4. Martha, Saint—Juvenile literature.
[1. Mary, of Bethany, Saint. 2. Martha Saint. 3. Bible stories—N.T.]
I. Jones, Dennis, ill. II. Title. III. Series: Simon, Mary Manz, 1948– Hear me read Bible stories.
BS2595.5.S45   1991
226.4'09505—dc20

90-46415
CIP
AC

04 05 06 07 08 09 10 11 12   09 08 07 06 05 04 03 02 01 00

Name _____

Date _____

Presented by _____

To the Adult:

Early readers need two kinds of reading. They need to be read to, and they need to do their own reading. The Hear Me Read Bible Stories series helps you to encourage your child with both kinds.

For example, your child might read this book as you sit together. Listen attentively. Assist gently, if needed. Encourage, be patient, and be very positive about your child's efforts.

Then perhaps you'd like to share the selected Bible story in an easy-to-understand translation or paraphrase.

Using both types of reading gives your child a chance to develop new skills and pride in reading. You share and support your child's excitement.

As a mother and a teacher, I anticipate the joy your child will feel in saying, "Hear me read Bible stories!"

Mary Manz Simon

To Jack Gerber
Psalm 127:1

Mary swept. Swish, swish, swish.

Martha cooked. Yum, yum, yum.

Mary and Martha worked,
worked, worked.

"Jesus will come," said Mary.

"Jesus will come here,"

said Martha.

Mary swept. Swish, swish, swish.

Martha cooked. Yum, yum, yum.

Mary and Martha worked.

"Come," said Mary.

"Jesus, Jesus," said Martha.

"Come," said Mary.

"Come and sit down.

Come and sit down here."

Jesus sat down.

Mary sat down.

Mary listened to Jesus.

Martha swept.

Swish, swish, swish.

Martha worked, worked, worked.

Mary listened to Jesus.

Martha cooked. Yum, yum, yum.

Martha worked, worked, worked.

Mary listened to Jesus.

Martha worked, worked, worked.

Martha sat down.

Mary listened to Jesus.

Martha said,

"Mary will not work.

Mary will not come and work."

Jesus said, "Come here, Martha.
Come and sit down."

Martha sat down.

Martha listened to Jesus.

Mary and Martha

listened to Jesus.

About the Author
Mary Manz Simon holds a doctoral degree in education with a specialty in early childhood education. She has taught at levels from preschool through postgraduate. Dr. Simon is the best-selling author of more than 40 children's books, including *Little Visits with Jesus*. She and her husband, the Reverend Henry A. Simon, are the parents of three children.